Stevenson

HEARTLANDS

Snapshots of a Grief

by

Steve Logan

'...to speak of the heart is not to sentimentalize but to ensoul'.'

(Thomas Moore)

First published in 2024

Moondragon Books

www.stevelogan.co.uk

Typeset by Kathryn Preston, Prestset Bureau

Printed in the EU via Akcent Media Limited

A CIP record of this book is available from the British Library

ISBN 978-1-913798-36-9

MIX

Paper from
responsible sources

FSC® C014138

In Memory of

Margaret Elizabeth Maggs, née Morgan

and

Philip Edward Maggs

Contents

Foreword
by
Pamela Petro

When I set out in 2012 to write my book, *The Long Field*, about the varied permutations of *hiraeth*, I began by reading what other writers had to say about this very Welsh sense of yearning—or nostalgia—or homesickness. It didn't take long. Very few writers had much to say about it at all. That is, until I found a pair of essays by Stephen Logan in the Welsh journal, *Planet*, which tackled the subject head-on.

'Looking at, and trying to see beyond, a line of hills is indeed a preparation for *hiraeth*,' writes Logan. And then he says how *hiraeth*, for him, clusters around '...the idea of home, and a sense of the divine just beyond the rim of perception, just beyond the brow of that next hill.'

Logan's words were keys that began to unlock the concept of unattainable longing for me—especially longing that's bedded down into real, physical places, grooved deep into memory. I thought to myself that there must be stories buttressing his words—stories and people and voices and valleys and love and rain and youth and loss—because that kind of understanding doesn't come from study. It only comes from acutely felt life.

As it happens, all of these things, and so much more, take centre stage in Steve (or Stephen) Logan's rich, holistically excavated, bravely rendered new poetry collection, *Heartlands*. These poems are the raw material from which his visual imagination distilled that brilliant image of *hiraeth* as the lodestar of our lives, forever slipping over the brow of the next hill. As such, they add up to nothing less than autobiography as conjured by a poet, musician, and Welshman (not necessarily in that order). The poems move from Logan's childhood in Wales to boarding school in England, then to Oxbridge academia: an arc that is anchored, above all, by the loving great-aunt and great-uncle with whom he lived as a child in Wales—a pair 'ensouled' by their nephew's poetry, to use Thomas Moore's phrase, rather than sentimentalized. It is to them that the collection is dedicated.

That Logan writes both of and for his aunt and uncle in the straightforward language of his Valleys youth, rather than the expected, cutting-edge cadences of contemporary poetry, is a rare act of both artistic freedom and emotional fidelity. Here is the tow-rope of *hiraeth* holding firm to the bedrock security of childhood. He addresses his aunt, 'less elegant than Whistler's mum— / Also less grim, thank God (you'd say, 'the Lord'),' quoting her own words, '*As happy as a dog with two tails*' to think of him, the poet, ''educated' now / Though still (those hills in these / Flatlands cupping my soul) / A son of Pontymister....'

There is an unfiltered intimacy here that I hadn't realized much contemporary poetry lacked until I read *Heartlands*. These poems are not performances of feeling. They are feelings themselves dressed in the language that best communicates with their subjects. We readers are onlookers, grateful to see love prove stronger than loss, over and over again, even as 'the soft, remembered tides / Of Porthcawl and Barry slacken through your veins,' as he writes to and about his dying aunt.

Here in this collection, too, are the wonders and terrors of daily life, celebrated with wit and gusto between joys, departures, and inevitable *hiraeth*. 'Harry the butcher with his devil's eye' and 'Old Mrs Moses shortsightedly marooned / In seas of uncharted ladieswear.' It says reams that in rooted images of remembered, dog-eared days, hearts don't leap into metaphor—they leap instead like the sturdy, necessary analogies they are: like 'that trout I caught / For Uncle's supper from the brook at Henllys.' When you have trout, who needs metaphors?

As Logan and the collection progress from Welsh hills and valleys to the plains of academia, the lens that Wales provided him with as a boy is never lost. The country and its *hiraeth* infuse everything from the clouds above Cambridge, reminiscent of his aunt's Welsh cakes, to consciousness itself, memorably referred to as 'the leafmould of the mind.' Reading *Heartlands* feels as familiar and natural to me as listening to my own thoughts, and I've revelled in the skill and humility required to render poetry so immediately recognizable to both head and heart. As for the soul, lodged somewhere in between, Logan isn't afraid to summon the old lodestar word outright. In the poem '*Hiraeth*, or Longing' he reassures the soul—this neediest yet most enigmatic aspect of ourselves—that 'God's voice echoes in the thought of home.' We are lucky to catch its cadences in this memorable collection.

Preface

People are of course more and other than the professions by which they are apt to be defined. I 'am', or work as, a musician, a poet, a psychotherapist and a university teacher in proportions that have varied through my life. These are just examples of the roles that we all adopt, fall into, or feel obliged to follow, choosing (if that is the word) from what happens to be available to us. Each role has its own stereotypes, opportunities and constraints. Multiple roles produce tensions which, for me, feel close to my creative centre: the currents of obscure energy I have tried in these poems to express.

The most obvious tension in the book has to do with my sense of cultural differences between South-East England and South-East Wales. There are associated class tensions. My father was a lorry driver by day and a club singer by night. Cambridge where I currently live is predominantly white, English and middle class. The valleys, where I grew up, were working class, with a strong idea that learning was not a middle class prerogative and a long tradition of spontaneous community support. The style of these poems is an expression of allegiance to the people I love, none of whom went to university and of whom some, like my great-uncle Philip, achieved their eloquence through being, not talking. Here is the source of another tension, since the literary world tends to identify wisdom (so far as such a thing is recognised) with verbal explicitness. One of the respects in which the culture I grew up in seems to me wise is that it maintained both a deep traditional respect for education and a wariness about the occasional provincialism of educated values.

I accept De Quincey's principle that a poem should provide its own explanation, while sensing this to be a counsel of perfection. Even in song-poetry—which occupies a position of cultural centrality page-poetry doesn't—it's common, indeed obligatory, to surround the work of any recognised songwriter with interviews, press-releases and social media titbits. The popularity of literary biography suggests that what most readers of page-poems now enjoy is neither the life nor the work in mutual isolation; but the life in relation to the work and the work in the context of the life. This is, after all, only restoring the condition of inter-relatedness which comes about anyway when a poet is well-known. Few poets read their poems without supplying a bit of what is rather surprisingly known as 'context'.

Accordingly, I have given a scattering of footnotes on personal names and place names which are significant to me, but which may to some readers be opaque. There are other notes on matters of biographical circumstance and on literary allusions. People who have read widely have often read very different things. For this reason I have sometimes given the sources of allusions and quotations which have been absorbed into my experience, but which may be of limited interest to others. I hope it will be obvious that that there is no question of these having been consciously inserted into the poems, least of all in an attempt to dignify the style. To do that would betray its purpose. The borrowed words arose from the same spring of feeling as the other words: a feeling for the domestic, moral, social, political and religious traditions of a specific place and time. Those heartlands led to these poems. As a Welshman, I hope these poems speak truthfully of qualities in the culture of the Valleys which are real and not just a private sentimental mirage. As a poet, I hope these poems recognise postmodernism and how to negotiate with it. As a musician, I hope these poems can sing.

Biography

Born among wirelesses when fathers wore
Ambition, like their Brylcreemed hair, cut short;
When mothers pined upon the never-never
And smothered innocence in cries of love.

Raised by an aunt, whose fruitless womb
Went undelivered of its child of pain;
Her husband gentle as the horses who
Whinnied through canyons of the rolling mill.

Ripped untimely from the womb of Wales,
Where farmlands dewy with solicitude
Wept warm colours into lesions of
Divorce. Then exile: boarding school

(Failure in despair); and university
(Success in desperation). Now,
Squirming on a bed of spires, he dreams
Of music good enough to write his life.

Guardian

Late Victorian; stripped pine: Cambridge.
Many original features, of course.
Yet your house, Aunt (my second mother)
Bearing, not boasting, the same quaint date
Was never so described.

Less *bijou*, 'Risca, near Newport, Gwent',
Land of my lissom, swarthy, fathers;
Unlettered in all but the mobility
Of our loved ones,
The stability
Of our loves.

Those rough-cut blocks
Of thirsty, facing stone:
Tossed up upon the music of a thousand chiming blasts
From just 'up the quarry', just above my school,
Just beneath my heart as it learnt the feel
Of its first local thumps and yearnings....

Uncle's ghostly granddad and his masons made,
There in Mill Street,
A pleasure-dome of sorts,[1]
Though such deeds never were to my ears then
Aspicked in allusions
I had yet to learn.

And you, less elegant than Whistler's mum—
Also less grim, thank God (you'd say, 'the Lord')—
How it grieves my cloven heart to think of you,
As happy as a dog with two tails
To think of me, 'educated' now
Though still (those hills in these
Flatlands cupping my soul)
A son of Pontymister,

---

[1] This and the preceding verse-paragraph allude to Coleridge's poem, 'Kubla Khan'. The house in Mill Street where I grew up was built by my great-uncle's grandfather.

Unwilling to replace
That bright wild cornflower of cliché,
Plucked from the valley of our childhood,
Which for me you wear
So jauntily
In the unexpectant whiteness
Of your hair.

Quiescence

To have reached the road's last turning and
Not know, when dusk, as soft as sootfall,
Spreads a veil across the mountains
That no sudden taunt of summer will again
Pester the thinning blood; no flash
Of autumn colour cause a stir
In the placid weather of the heart...

To sit and watch and wait and feel
As memories glimmer past the mind's closing doors,
That this is all: these rooms, these kindly
Strangers' voices, these cut flowers
Bought in haste
Or sad deliberation—all
That's still in store, that's yet to come,

Can seem for those of us still toiling up
Or down the ragged slopes of time,
Time's sole, tear-sodden recompense.

Family gone, friends long overboard,
Names and faces fading—
Only the cemetery among the hills
A bright spot in your heart, my love,
Whose smile is now so heavenly
With pathos.

Double Absolution

Nothing I want more, at this moment—
The stolid bricks of a Cambridge terrace
Balking my outward vision—
Than to heave my helpless heart into my mouth
And kiss your poor life better.
I had a dream last night, you'd breathed your last
Unheeded sigh. The brittle pages of the book
In which I've sought through many weary years
A sentence of acquittal suddenly
Blanched, the cantilevers of resolve
Let fall my arched ambition and,
As I wept through vortexes of the night,
I heard your voice grown young again
Piercing the tantrums of your later years.
You said: 'No need to reassure me now.
I take the apple of your childish love,
Wrap it in a fold of these warm Welsh hills
And burnish it to brightness. Then,
With one clean bite across my own reflection,
I summon all the succour that I came to crave,
And spread myself eternally at ease among the stars.'
With that I woke, the taste of double absolution
Easing, like dock leaves from the Welfare,[2]
The smart of waking tears.

---

[2] Name of the local recreation ground. Among children I knew, dock leaves with spit on them were a favoured remedy for nettle-stings.

So Long

Adrift on a bed at St. Woolos,[3]
Now, as the soft, remembered tides
Of Porthcawl and Barry[4] slacken through your veins;
As clouds from Twmbarlwm[5] shield the eyes
Which have watched and wept beneath his silent brow;
As you gather tight to your unsuckled breasts
Blankets of the rippling fields
Your feet felt their first young grass in;

All that's needed is for you to take
A deep impression of the valley's sheltering warmth—
Each shop along Commercial Street[6]
Replete with your remembrances:
Harry the butcher with his devil's eye;
Jack Jones's always so handy and so dear;
Old Mrs Moses shortsightedly marooned
In seas of uncharted ladieswear;
And the green Bazaar where you magicked me
Trinkets from the Orient, even if that meant
Nowhere more exotic than Newport or Cardiff...

Just nuzzle your exhausted cheek
Into the shadows of the mountainside
Your mother danced her youth in
(While you took whirling steps to follow her);
And, crumpling every fruitless hope
Into a sigh as lissom as the touch
Of the lover's hand your body dreamed
Would harvest all your womanhood;
Fill with draughts of love too deep for pain
The heart I would swaddle in a manger full
Of poetry and prayer, before you kiss
This world and me one last good-bye.

---

[3] A hospital in Newport, South Wales.
[4] Cheap and cheerful holiday resorts on the South Welsh coast.
[5] A mountain which is to Pontymister what Helvellyn is to Grasmere and visible from my great aunt's house.
[6] The main shopping street between Pontymister and Risca, running along the valley-floor.

Gifts

Your birthday and your favourite time of year:
The trees hold up frail blossoms to the spring;
Each day's a first: you would have loved to hear
The sparrows finding out what they can sing.

You never wanted much: 'Just bring yourself',
You'd tell me every time I offered more;
Your smile and your indifference to pelf
Enriched me as I reached your open door.

The tantrums and the fierce reclusiveness
That made you want to 'bite a nail in two'
Were livid streaks in what I none the less
Loved as the pearl that gave its name to you.[7]

The flowers on your grave I didn't pull:
My hands are empty, Aunt; my heart is full.

---

[7] The name 'Margaret' comes, via French *Marguerite* and Latin *Margarita*, from the Greek word for 'pearl' (μαργαρίτης [margarítēs]). This has long seemed to me a significant fact about Hopkins's poem, 'Spring and Fall' and for me links his 'Margaret' with my great-aunt. As a priest he would of course have been familiar with the parable of 'the pearl of great price' (Matthew 13:45-6). It came to strike me my great-uncle's way of honouring his wife's full value that he rarely abbreviated her name.

Chronology

In the 'Chronology' I tabulate his life:[8]
What he published, where he lived and when
He married, came into money, grieved.
Eighty years takes just five pages. Yet
Even within so tight a grid—perhaps
Because of it—his pain,
The whole molten mantle of emotion
That heaves beneath the contours of each life
Strains and agitates the armature.

Coolly, I note that Wordsworth,
Two months absent from his home
And after eight years of marriage, 'writes
Many passionate letters to his wife.'
The stolid typeface glows.
But then I add, more briefly still:
'Daughter Catherine dies, aged 3;
Son Thomas dies, aged 6' and
In a mist that suffuses the table
Of dates I see my Guardian's eyes,
(Before they opened to eternity) flood
With all a lifetime's tears.
                                              You had
Asked me to summarize Wordsworth's life—
Taking an interest in my work—but when
I came to Daughter Catherine you wept,
As if I had been eloquent. But no.
How great your sorrow must have been—
Obscured by its very ordinariness—when
You learned that I, adopted
By your barren womb,
Was being after ten years' dream of motherhood
Reclaimed.

            It isn't only in the flesh
That death can plunge its ice-hot hands.
You had died a dozen times before
Time took your brain and opened up a crack
Just to relieve the gathered sorrow
Slowly smothering your heart.

---

[8] Written while compiling a 'Chronology' of Wordsworth's life for an edition of his poems.

Bridge of Sighs

You loved bridges, so I gave you this:
A picture of a famous, Lakeland bridge
In a cheap tin frame. Five inches by six,
Its details must have been invisible
From where you used to sit, alone.

                                 And yet
Each time throughout the hopeless day,
When you moved, as in another person's dream,
Across the living room, replete with relics
Of all my former ages, I can feel
How your straining eyes would catch, perhaps,
The colour of the grass, or brook, or stone,
And, just before you cracked the stiff brown door
(Which never got the easing that it needed)
And lost all recollection
Of what you'd gone in search of,
Your heart would have leapt, like that trout I caught
For Uncle's supper from the brook at Henllys[9]
And, climbing through the spray, have turned into
The rainbow bridge which now I walk across, towards you.

---

[9] Name of a village, pronounced, in the part of South-East Wales where it stands, '*ent*-luss'

Lakelands

Deep, lonely, inaccessible
As the remotest pent-up tarn;
Its kinship only with the bounding sky
That it mirrors, melts and mars,

Your suffering tumbles the son in me
Down sudden gulfs of grief,
When, at the top of some scree'd ascent
I bluster into vision

Of you, dissolving slowly on the skiff
Of an unmoved hospital bed:
You who were once a slip of a girl
With hair that glistened like split coal,

And eddied like the stream at Henllys where
I caught that lunging trout. The waters
Lap me cold, yet they're warm
As tears with all the past.

This morning I am sodden
With lakelands of regret.
Our final holiday breakfast and
Into fathoms where pity waits

The radio casts 'I can't
Stop loving you.' The line
Twists through me like the road to Risca,
Where you no longer live.

I love you so much how could I
Long to see these distant fells
Rise above their grief, if that should mean
Leaving you behind?

Tang of Autumn

For Philip Edward Maggs

This morning autumn, waking from a dream
Of summer's love-sobs in a sheet of cloud,
Took me captive with its dewy eye,
And led me to the very brink
Of memory. In our own back garden,
Plums plump for amethyst amid the green
Gloom of 'arbours'. The elder preens
And sprigs itself with annual reminders
(Wet and vivid as a sparrow's eye)
Of wine we drank in prospect, but never made,
In the glad, shabby groves of infancy. I fetch
My bike from the shed and taste the tang
Of something in the sunlight, teasing the tip
Of recollection; a softness nestling in the cool
Of winds that frisk and tumble through the breaking
Years. It lifts my longing to the moment's brim
And tells me: 'Drink'.

                    The atmosphere
Reams with promise. Fragrancies of fern
Nimbling through the dirt-tracks of Ochrwyth;[10]
The Ebbw's[11] plashy pockets stuffed full
Of trout and pebbles; tall spear-grass
Cocking its ear for shoes of men and horses;
And one horse in particular which you, Philip[12]
(Lover of horses you could never own),
Led to the garden of The Farmers' Arms,
One night in all your gentleness with me.
There, with light-bulbs green and amethyst
Setting easy limits to a patch of heaven,
That shadowy horse—for me the father of all horses,
Whose gleaming muscles tense each time
I mention 'fetlock', 'flank' or 'bridle'—
Bows her head to the grass where now
Your ashes twinkle like your eyes
As we stood in paradise above our valley
And you in silence slugged your pint.
Drunk with autumn, we sank our roots
Into the earth where poems grow.

---

[10] An area on the lower slopes of Machen mountain, south-west of Risca, which is locally referred to as 'The Big Wood'. Pronounced '*ooker-weeth*' (the first word rhyming with cooker.)

[11] This river runs under a bridge we used to cross when leaving Pontymister, to enter the Big Wood.

[12] The name 'Philip' means 'lover of horses' (from φιλ ἵππος [*phil hippos*]).

Any Road

A child, of course I never wished or tried
To fathom his plain mystery. It was
The element in which I lived and moved
As equably I flexed my strength against
His frank, inscrutable grown-upness.

At night, when he'd been working afternoons,
I'd stare seven years' defiance at
My own engulfing sleepiness, then,
From underneath the blanket of its breakers, be
Woken from my vigil by the soft salute
Of his baritone cough, and the clippering
Of ageing hobnails on the ancient flags.

There was a hole in the left side of his neck—
A sort of navel. I never knew
How he came by it. If God had placed
A finger there to draw imagination up
An umbilical cord to heaven, neither He
Nor Uncle—eyes trained on the earth—ever told.
Uncle, at any rate, *couldn't* have.
I never met a man to whom his native tongue
Was more profoundly hieroglyphic;
The Woodbine in his mouth more like a burning coal
Some angel awed him into silence with.

And so his nickname 'Fly' remained
A fossil lodged forever in his past.
I am no wiser now, except about the love
He struck like sparks out of the furnace in the loft,
Blew upon each morning I watched him light the fire,
And which I carry molten in my veins,
Like steel in runnels of the rolling mill,
Or mirth in barrels at the Myrtle Inn.[13]

---

[13] Name of a pub in Pontymister. The Rolling Mill, another pub nearby, took its name from the local steelworks, where my great-uncle earned his living.

Emerging from a paper-shop tonight,
Miles apart from the mountains that looked down
On all my childhood Christmases,
I felt myself as deeply drenched in wonders
As his old jacket in varieties of smoke
From steelworks, garden-fire, pub, or marriage.
Now, inside of all the mysteries
I once believed he knew the secret of,
My footsteps echo his along a road that leads
Into a silence singing with strange light,
Where longing finds its voice and its fulfilment.

Even so, I half-expect to find him there,
Elbows resting on his knees, his cap
Cosseting his balding, Brylcreemed head,
Looking up baffled from my poems, saying:
'You got here at last, my son, any road.'

Cowboys

Sixty five, laid off at Llanwern,[14]
Wheezing on forty Woodbines a day,
He never paused an instant before—
Book in the hand he maimed for me
Sledgehammering up a garden swing—
He leapt astride the tall bay stallion
And mounted the lonely ridge.

There, out among horizons broader
Than Risca hills held in their sweet lasso,
He faced the raw Kimanche, knew
The ways of Blackfoot, Cheyenne, Sioux,
Herded buffalo, bison and
The wild,
Wild horses
Of the scorched Arizona canyons.

Then, his work behind him, he
Sloped down gently to his homestead in the Valleys,
Where his wife cooked dinner good as prairie stew
And I, his lone adopted son, watched wide-eyed
As (touching my heart in conspiracies of love)
He shook the warm, exotic sand
Out of his turn-ups, looked straight ahead
And tightened invisible reins.

Turning in my desk-chair now,
I hear the creak of saddle-leather,
Taste the salt winds blowing directions
Across the pathless plains.

---

[14] Site of a steelworks, east of Newport, to which my great-uncle was transferred following the closure of the steelworks at Pontymister.

Humility, or the Common Room[15]

Bald heads I wouldn't care about,
Bad teeth or shabby clothes;
The shuffle, stoop, or ink stains:
One I love had all of those—
Apart from ink stains.

　　　　　But when he returned
His Westerns to the library and laboriously
Wrote 'P' (for Philip), 'E' (for Edward), 'M' (for Maggs),
Inside each one of hundreds, he'd no thought
Of embezzling the glory of his 'betters':
Men who wrangled herds of words
Through fertile deltas of his lowland mind,
Or helped him write the cast-list for
A million formulaic show-downs,
As the coal ricocheted up the chimney.

Perhaps he never even wondered, while
His Woodbines [16] wreathed their gunsmoke
Round fingers delicately cradling his book
(As it might be a child, as it might be me)
Whether being 'educated' wouldn't be a boon.

Oh, *then* he could tell his dreams
To scholars who, fallen angels in old clothes,
Would see, in the wonder of his trustful eyes,
Corrals full of promise, mountains that rose
Above opportunity's horizons,
And a shack where the likes of Virgil and Homer
Tipped their Stetsons to a man who knew
Something more important than their names.

---

[15] See Yeats's poem, 'The Scholars' ('Bald heads forgetful of their sins...').
[16] My great-uncle's favourite brand of cigarette.

Heartlands

'Don't grow too big round here, do they?'
He looked into his raddled palm
Like a schoolboy at a beaten conker.
Clearly the stunted blackberries had seemed
All right to him beforehand. He gazed
A moment, willing their shrivelled amplitude
To plump itself back up, indifferent to the wind
Of a stranger's thoughtlessness. 'Maybe it's the chalk',
I added, anxious to atone, my foot
Still treading on the home-made mythologies
That house our hearts. 'Maybe', he half-retorted;
'But I've been coming here forty years
And don't recall them any bigger.' His eyes,
Grey and rheumy, like a fen in mist,
Suddenly waxed waterlogged with all the griefs
That berry-picking stemmed. The conjunction of
His bright checked shirt and youth-drained skin
Was now, in the way that casual talk
Protects us from quite seeing, vibrantly
Pitiful: his blackberrying a clue to some
Sad, stubborn hope of continuity stretched
Out towards his self of forty years ago,
When time and the deaths had not yet
Strangled his boyish treble.

                              'What are these?'—
I blundered on, entangling myself
Still further, like a preoccupied dog
Wrapping his lead around a post. 'Are they
Sloes?' 'Yes, sloes.' I was glad of his
Corroboration: now Dylan's words
('sloeblack, slow, black')[17] could take on flesh;
And, for a moment, the stern and chalky fens
Sucked in softness like a mothering eye
And shook their unrelenting flatness into
Luscious folds of mountainside,
Where childhood berries gorged themselves
On Welsh soil drunk with rain.

---

[17] '...the sloeblack, slow, black, crowblack, fishingboat-bobbing sea.' Dylan Thomas, from the
second sentence of *Under Milk Wood* (1953).

Happy, as I hadn't been for hours before—
Despite the wilful education of my heart
To graze on cloudscapes in default of mountains—
I ventured one more step. 'And aren't
Sloes the earliest of berries?' (I had confused
The blackthorn's berries with its blossom). The Fenman came
Back waveringly into view. 'Well...', he began,
Again subduing his retort, 'They're the last
To go at Christmas.' The momentary
Mist of confusion above the grief
In his eyes gently lifted; and, as the land
Regained its proper level, I beheld
A clump of berries from the valleys thrive
In the chalky flatlands of his flesh.

Hiraeth, or Longing[18]

The word's a stranger to my tongue. It cleaves
To warlords dank with history, or
Ghostly shepherds trudging through
The clabber of ages, the battered heart's
Compass needling them on.

                              But these
Frail wraiths have passed its meaning down,
Their hands dissolving as they touch
The hearts of each inheritor: my Aunt,
Fresh back from servitude in London, feeling
Her mother come to meet her as she eyed the hills
Where Uncle—bolted to the valley-floor
By chains of British Steel—now rides
The horses that entranced him in the betting-shop;
And me, as mountains rise above the page
Of a Welsh poet's *Autobiographies*, sending,
Bottled in a poem, these immemorial tears:
Dark as eyes in anguish; scalding bright
As hospital corridors after death;
And wayward as the passages of time.

Soft through valleys of each exiled heart,
Bruised with longing by the stars that tell
Of silent forbears languishing east,
God's voice echoes in the thought of home.

---

[18] '*hiraeth*: a Welsh word traditionally felt to be not susceptible to adequate translation. Its general meaning is "longing"—especially longing for a native place and culture left behind, or felt to be irretrievable.' R. S. Thomas, *Autobiographies,* ed. Jason Walford Davies (London: J. M. Dent, 1997), p. 179.

Mangle

The scrunched and gawping lager cans
Sprawl across the yard, among
Lighters the colour of old boiled sweets—
Like the ones my other aunt displayed
On her hand as if they'd been the holy host—[19]
Condoms (probably) and, for all I know,
Hypodermic gateways to
A heaven mostly sneered at.

Tussocks of grass and dandelions—
'I'm like a lion'—ruffed with shaving-soap
He'd say, and she, before the jokes left home
Quipped back, 'Aye, a *dande*lion— sprout
Dejectedly between the flags
As though they mourned the absence of
The fingers that in widowed loneliness
Curbed their indecorum.

This yard is now an emblem of
A culture partly indisposed
To put away its waste, although
It builds old people's 'homes' upon
The rubble of broken families
And hasn't got time to honour
Lives in their final ruin.

Here once I saw the glistering perfection
Of my first childhood snow. It was as if
Winter shook itself awake
And brought white sky to earth.
Here too my uncle (lion enough I thought)
Fashioned me a bike-stand out of bits of wood
And the love that set me on a saddle, riding
A ruby steed they'd bought on tick from Curry's,
Sublimely unconscious of his hand
As it loosed into freedom the saddle and me.

At one end stood a snowy rose bush where
The cat I'd begged her to take in

---

[19] The name of the Aunt (strictly, great-aunt) who brought me up was Margaret. (See 'Gifts'). The 'other Aunt', her sister Mary, lived 3 miles away in Rogerstone. She was full of boisterous good humour, was verbally spellbinding and was always ready to hand out sweets. Their parents evidently had a sense of the poetry of names, since the third of these sisters, my grandmother, was 'Martha'.

Had gone to die below the flowers
That climbed like a flock of angels up
And down across a crescent frame,
Their heads heavy with rain. I see
My aunt in black and white framed
Within this fragrant arch:
A plump and pinnied[20] Venus
With a sword piercing her heart for me.

At the other end, the wash-house: merely
A flat tin roof on top of four vanished walls
Where Uncle, in old brogues and baggy trousers
Strove against the wind to catch a signal for
The aerial he'd created in homage to the God
Of chapels he visited twice a year,
While Aunt in the 'kitchen' (our living room) nearby
Would fiddle, full of prayers and curses, with the set.
Inside the wash-house hung the old tin bath
Where tiny miners like myself
Cruised, at uncertain intervals, before
An open fire; also there
Were tubs of spuds and sudden spiders.

On summer days I'd nimble up
Onto the sun-blanched corrugated roof,
And, as the warmth sank through my frame
I'd close my eyes and see the flagstones glowing
Gold beneath my feet, the whole back yard
Translated into Eden.

Now he's disappeared beyond
His final solitary frontier
And she soon stumbled after, losing
More of the mind that mothered me,
Crying 'O Lord, help me, O dear, O dear';
And what I see in the yard is this
Unmemoried sacrilege of intruders:
A broken window in whose fragments are
Reflected the smashed heavens of the psalms;
And an old mangle which she would never let
The scrap-man have: its tight lips bleached
With suffering, its iron strength
Spent and yet, and yet and yet
Trying to tell its tale of all
The life that once went through it.

---

[20] Wearing a pinny, pinafore or apron.

Apocalypse

Christmas fog spangling the moon-struck sky,
Fearless and trembling, I set my foot
On a tarmacked road that took me up
Somewhere nearer innocence. Beneath,
The sad world aching dreamed.

Nineteen winters had led up to this.
I heard the frosted gravel crash like sea
On the shingled childhood of my bones.
Jumping jacks of hawthorn stung the air
And made it freshly wonder. Knowingly
Oaks and yews leafed back through all their ages.
Moments merged into a stream on which
The fraught mind merely drifted, when
The bracken rustled red alert
And dawn broke into flame.

The god of Machen[21] heaved a boiling sun
Onto his shoulder, then spilled out a sack
Of intimations right across the fields.
Leaning back to contemplate, he watched
As sheep, meaning nothing less marvellous than themselves,
Through depths of light unfocused loomed
Gently into vision, and the bright
Living bible of the mountainside
In one soft sermon, wordlessly Welsh,
Read its theology into my blood.

---

[21] The mountain between Risca and Machen village which I walked up over one Christmas morning.

Edges

Once, the world I lived in had no edges:
That six-mile strip of valley-floor
With sides that yearned beyond themselves
Was all of it: a poem where, footloose,
I metred out uncounted days,
Laid anxiety to sleep and sang
The countersong of my emotions
Into harmony with woods, lanes, bikes,
School and the flagstones of our own back yard.

There, I could stretch my spirit like a cat
And soak the colour of the weather in:
Bakestone Junes; Christmases
That hung globes in windows;
Autumns muskily ripening
The bruised and vibrant fruits of spring.
The air and my unknown self
Had a single contour. There was no place
This world wouldn't try to swallow,
Each patch of wilderness a match for home.

And then as everyone older knew
Time drew up quite unannounced,
Slinging the unreality of elsewhere
Into a box of broken toys and, lockjawed,
Waited to meet me. Other places
Beat against the inside of the TV screen
And, all unnoticed, began their slow
Crash into my fields of vision.

My mother's voice faintly calling from London
Grew loud and took my heart in hand.
One summer's day, fresh from hunting
Perch and roach and flame-finned rudd,
I found myself, as never again,
Clueless among perplexities:
A ten-year-old in a phone-box choosing
Between the home I had in Risca
And one I might have somewhere else.
A desperate desire for integration
Cracked wholeness apart and flung
Its fragments to the ends of a new world
Where horizons glimmer
Like guillotines; like tears.

Hill of Dreams

Past shattered skies of longing,
Punched black and blue with night,
I chased a ghost of feeling
Widely considered trite;

Through dismal skies of morning
I redefined a hill
Plump with dreams lost children
Take some time to kill;

And far behind my eyelids,
Where truth makes up its face,
My hill stood drenched with acid rain
Dropped out of empty space;

In a sentimental reflex
I give the image one last kiss
Then turn back to the TV news
Waving good-bye to Idris Davies.[22]

---

[22] Idris Davies (1905-53) is a currently unsung working-class Welsh poet, from Rhymney, eighteen miles north of Risca. From fourteen till twenty-one, he worked as a miner then, following a hand-injury, took correspondence courses and became a poet. In response to many mining disasters in South-East Wales, Davies wrote 'The Bells of Rhymney', which The Byrds made famous in their 1965 song—a setting of the poem by Pete Seeger. Both in this and in Seeger's own recording, 'Rhymney is mispronounced (the first syllable should be *rum* not *rim*). When Davies's book, *Gwalia Deserta*—a kind of Welsh *Waste Land*—was published by T. S. Eliot in 1938, it got a dismissive review in Geoffrey Grigson's *New Verse*. Seeing this, Davies wrote a magisterial defence of his apparently simple and non-progressive style, pointing out that he would have felt it wrong to write about miners in the language of Auden and Spender. This sense of a style needing in some way to be answerable to the people it commemorates is one I share.

Learning by Heart

Among these leaves I dare not linger long
Lured and lapped by the lullaby of songs
That murmured through the mountains of my youth:
'Gloire de Dijon', 'Cherry-Robbers', 'Sorrow'
And 'Song of a Man who Has Come Through'.[23]
The petals of their titles drift wistfully down
On rivers that weren't memory then;
But the strong meandering waters
Of a life in its chequered spring.

Twenty years on, tumbling rapids behind me—
Slow eddies, too, in which hopeless love,
Anchored in yearning, hid from the current
As time skiffed murderously on—
A ghost, like myself at seventeen,
Emerges from a date in the book's front cover.
Some kid from the valleys, uprooted, lost—
The props of his affections[24] in a distant hill—
Begs dumb books for an analgesic.

I watch my slender, transient frame
Drift through St. John's Wood churchyard, dreaming
Lines of cool comfort from Larkin, Enright, Davie,
Or sucking on the sap of Heaney's warmer, gutteral muse.
The blood of all three bardic Thomases[25]
Echoed down my veins until,
Exiled in a classroom, reading Hughes's 'Pike',
And fishing for Wales, I saw soft waters darken
· And a float, unconscious of its loneliness,
Slid away into depths whose significance I knew.

I see my own unmolested face
As if it was my son's. Its eyes
Trustful, eager, quick and keen,
Grow quietly unbelieving, then
Cloud over irresistibly,
Adrift in tears we all must shed
From pain peculiar to ourselves.
I, helpless, moon[26] above the depths
Of other poems, lives not mine.

---

[23] Poems I first read in Keith Sagar's selection from Lawrence's poems, which I bought aged 17.
[24] See *The Prelude* (1805), ii. 294. Wordsworth's phrase refers to his parents, both of whom he
lost while young.
[25] Edward, Dylan and R.S..
[26] Cp. 'I fruitless mourn' in Thomas Gray's 'Sonnet on the Death of Richard West'.

Lost in Woods

My blood is blended with the sap
That thrills and thrums along the limbs
Of every Lady of the Wood[27]
Who tells her love in falling leaves.

When I lean against a tree
And feel its age seep into mine,
The sway of my emotion takes
Its measure from the stars that shine

Above the mantle of the wood:
They wink at impulses that stir
In penetralia of the mind[28]
Where childhood voices whisper and murmur.

And when I stretch my hand against
The cloud-sustaining blue I see
Among my bones the roots that rise
From the dark unconscious of each tree

Housing the forest birds that flit
From thought to branching thought and sing
Threnodies to the autumn light
That sets my timber echoing.

---

[27] In 'The Picture, or The Lover's Resolution', Coleridge, describes the silver birch as 'the Lady of the Woods'—a name said to be from Celtic folklore. I probably picked it up from Edward Thomas, writing about Willian Cobbett.

[28] See Keats's letter to George and Tom Keats, 21 December 1817: 'Coleridge, for instance, would let go by a fine isolated verisimilitude caught from the Penetralium of mystery, from being incapable of remaining content with half knowledge.'

Celts

'Welshman, yes?' 'Caernafon. You?'
'Newport.' 'That's not Wales'
The lilt on which my speech is strung
Knows where it's from.

His confidence secures itself
By hawsers of an ancient tongue
To soil that North, West, East and South
Possess in unison.

The Book of Kells:[29] a work of hands
Whose art had only faith to quell
The supplicating guts beneath
The board, served the lands

That make a rumpled tricorn of
The loyalties that bind them, then
Refine upon each point with clans
Of Scotland, Wales and Ireland.

Some wise urchin blazoned on
A wall in Belfast: 'If you're not
Confused you don't understand.'
I'm confused, of course, so can't

Forget a film in black and white
Unsheathed one lunchtime from a vault:
It ran my eyeball through and roused
Some fictive Celt to arms.

---

[29] A district in County Meath, Leinster, site of a monastery whose scribes are associated with the production, during the eighth or ninth century, of an illuminated copy of the Gospels in Latin. The beauty of the book suggests—in this case at least—the interrelatedness of high artistic achievement, piety, religious tradition and national culture.

A boy of maybe seven in
A South Welsh playground, not at play,
A placard round his neck to say
He'd dared to speak in Welsh.[30]

He was my father's father.
Newport water made his heart
Soft enough to feel a shame
Instilled by Whitehall art.

And so to hear this man from hills
Higher up in Wales reprove
Our Southern lack of loyalty—
The Celt within me quails.

Soul of Dai ap Gwilym
Born again in R. S. Thomas
Did you think that Dylan's softness meant
The Welsh had gone out from us?

---

[30] From as early as 1798, children in some schools in Wales were discouraged from using the Welsh language. After 1847 especially, when the government in Whitehall published a report ascribing educational backwardness in Wales in part to the currency of Welsh, the practice developed of hanging a small board, known as the 'Welsh Not' around the neck of any child heard speaking it. There is some debate about how widespread this practice actually was. While working in a college of further education in Huntingdon, I met a woman from the same valley as myself but much older. She remembered a schoolfriend in Risca, which was almost entirely English-speaking by my time, who had limited English. A sad paradox is that the areas of Wales most susceptible to government interference and to work-related immigration— such as brought my father's grandfather to Newport from Cork—are by some regarded as less Welsh than areas further west and north. National purity is, in my view, a reckless fantasy. National identity, however, is real.

Nostalgia

What does it mean to love
A person, place or thing?
That man's easy competence; the line
Against her cheek of that woman's hair;
The blend of clarity and open-hearted grace
In a well-intentioned sentence, or

The sound, now, of a fireplace
Lapping gas-fed tongues of flame
Over coals that, forty years ago
Would have been real—would have been
Laid in the grate by my great-aunt Margaret
(My guardian, always just 'Aunt' to me)
And brought in a scuttle by 'Uncle' Philip
From the coal-shed which, like the wash-house next to it,
Is now a thing of the past.

Some day, perhaps, work will begin
On the house that I grew up in,
So badly derelict that memory must preserve
The forms our lives (more frailly than we knew)
Retained under the shadow
Of the Pontymister mountains. Why
Should it matter? A billion living things
This very day will, unperceived,
Sink into the soil and make to time
A gift of the music of their molecules.

There are tears in this: tears that run
Deep as the secrets in every human soul—
Restorative, corrosive, inscrutable—
Even, or most of all, to ourselves;
Secrets like habits that we learned as kids
Among specific people, places, things;
And when we shed our first unnoticed
Tears of loss, invisibly as rain
They sink into our surroundings, nourishing
The roots of remembered beauty
From the springs of forgotten pain.

Empson in Peking

Not for me.[31] However many faces local
Buddhas might disclose in their compassion.[32] Whatever
The relief of having to make do with books
Disencumbered of scholarly apparatus
Purged of vitriol and freed up from sham finesse.

True, the manners would be nice. Even if the smiles
Dimpling towards me from unreadable lips
Translated into ideograms of isolation,
They'd be a touch less deadly than
Cambridge glumness and deflection
Of the apprehensive eye.

                But no; one day
Ensconced with sunlight in the floating world
Of rented flats, and ties too quickly
Made to hold—the windows high
Above the restless street, the electric fan
Turning impassively as the air grew dank
With emptiness—there, on the cover of a book
Like this I'd see some entirely unremarkable
Reproduction of a rural scene;[33]
And somewhere in the distance, way across the flats,
The spire of an English church would skewer
My new illusions as I recalled, within its nave,
Flung on an unfrequented pew,
A letter from my father (younger then than me)
Postmarked 'Northampton', singing like Mayday
Out towards the ancient, listening hills of Wales,
And telling a story I still strain to hear.[34]

---

[31] William Empson (1906-84) was for some years (1937-9; 1947-52) a Professor of English at Peking National University.

[32] Empson wrote an article, 'The Faces of Buddha' (*The Listener*, 5 February 1936) and possibly a longer essay, now lost, on the same subject. The article is reprinted in *Argufying: Essays on Literature and Culture*, ed. John Haffenden (London: Chatto and Windus, 1987), pp. 573-6.

[33] A 1995 Penguin edition of Empson's book, *Some Versions of Pastoral* (1935) has on its cover a picture showing a distant church-spire above the horizon of a flat (possibly Dutch) landscape.

[34] My father, whom I had seen little of during my childhood, died aged 40, just as I was getting to know him.

Exile

Walking through the court
(As Cambridge quads are called)
Sometimes I'd feel the air
Turn suddenly thick and hoops
Of hopelessness enclose
My silting, homeless lungs.[35]

The redbrick College walls[36]
Bore me no grudge: I trusted
Their impassivity,
While yearning for the love
Of one who filled a father's
Absence with a dream
Of truth become a beauty
Intellect might win.

The stone of Oxford Colleges
Was like a biscuit golden
With atmospheres of thought
Absorbed from C. S. Lewis:
The streets were deep in talk
I had with those who shared
His vision of a life
Where each true scholar was
An exile of the spirit
Seeking a way back home.

To Cambridge then I came[37]
And found the social climate
Marble-cool and yet
Those eighteenth-century windows
Were fine if they could frame
An image of Donald Davie smiling:[38]

---

[35] After living for ten years in Oxford, followed by a three-year return to South Wales, I took up an academic job in Cambridge.

[36] Of Selwyn College, Cambridge.

[37] Cp. 'To Carthage then I came'. The Waste Land, l. 307.

[38] English poet and critic (1922-95). Davie was much interested in the ideas of 'purity' and 'chastity' of style. His first book was called *Purity of Diction in English Verse* (1952). He wrote a severely self-critical poem called 'Revulsion' about not being able to stomach what he saw as gratuitous ugliness in some contemporary writing. He admired Wordsworth for carrying 'sobriety of outlook' into 'the very minutiae of poetic style'. And, seeing my estrangement from the world that I was in, he was kind to me.

Their fluted architraves
Suggest how sun could run its fingers
With fatherly tact over the stone
As his mind might feel the figure
Of a chaste Augustan ode.

But should the sunlight yield
To the psychic undertow
And flinch with premonition
Of others I could name
(Whose words impale their wisdom
On skewers of hidden need),
Then at once these academic
Bowers would be ransacked
With foreboding; Each page
Of scholarly endeavour
Gone 'stale and sicklied o'er'.

Forge Hammer, Rolling Mill,
And Myrtle[39]—stations on
The road that echoes through
The heartlands of the past;
If I could only hear
Welsh voices sing their prose
Within the holts and hollows
Of the wood that homes my heart
The page would be illumined
Where strangers write strange truth:
All will be well, all manner of things
Often so ill, will be well.[40]

---

[39] Pubs along Commercial Street, Pontymister, which I passed on my way to school.

[40] See *Four Quartets*, 'Little Gidding', sect. V. Eliot's line alludes to a passage in *Sixteen Revelations of Divine Love* by the 14th century mystic Julian of Norwich: 'Sin is behovely [of some use or unavoidable]; but all shall be well and all shall be well and all manner of thing shall be well.'

Homeliness

My first good essay as an undergraduate
(Schooling myself once more to feel at home)
Was on the character of homeliness
Cwtched[41] up in the pages of Orwell's prose.

I still recall the hearth-warm ache
Of recognition at his vignettes of
'Father' in an armchair after Sunday roast
By a crackling fire watching the newsprint wooze.[42]

How could I have known that decades on
My poems would yearn across the same horizons,
Feeling out a path through Oxford, London, Newport,
To a house, now vanished, on the far side of a hill;

Or that the 'children's voices at the end of lanes'[43]
Included one, my own, which I had lost?

---

[41] *Cwtch* is current as a noun and verb throughout Wales. To cwtch means 'to cuddle in an easy-going but especially affectionate way.' It is much used by mothers, of course, and is accordingly rich in associations from the first moments of consciousness. 'Cwtching up' means to snuggle in the hope of getting an affectionate and warming cuddle, or 'cwtch'. The 'w' stands for the same vowel as in English RP 'put'.

[42] See the opening paragraph of George Orwell's essay, 'Decline of the English Murder' (1946).

[43] My recollection of a line I seem to remember Seamus Heaney quoting in a radio interview. He said he'd written it, liked it, but hadn't been able to find a home for it.

Academic History

Leaves and folios in deepest groves
Of sequestration: all the talk
Among the bookish etymologies
Is rich with rural calm, or else—
Like 'Athenaeum' and 'Academy'—
Dappled with the civic ease
Of sunlight on tooled bindings.
(There is a coolness in the sound of 'vale').[44]

Not that there were no wrangles—what
Sucked the vigour out of Socrates
Wasn't merely hemlock but
The hate that stirred it. Nonetheless,
Pauline strifes were gendered in
The loins of appetite for knowledge, real
As fruit, palpable as faith or a fall,
And free of self-inverted commas.

Here once the sages of antiquity,
Whose dreams were rigorous from depth of love,
Paced out their propositions and
Sought truth in coverts of the questing eye.
Here masters of the village school,
Whose chalky hands might once have steered
A plough, or shaken compost from
The gleaming troves beneath each haulm,
Find now a drier succulence
Under blue Odyssean skies, or cliffs
Hung with Virgilian purples.

In the modern university, among
Stacks bulging with the withered gourds
Of the last research assessment exercise,
Practitioners of the humanities
Practice avoiding each other's eyes;
And, deconstructing 'wisdom' as
A sentimental ideology,
Swaddle their aching empty chests
In the grave clothes of metalanguage.

---

[44] Alongside the phrase, 'the vales of Heaven', in *Paradise Lost*, i. 321, Keats wrote 'There is a cool pleasure in the very sound of vale.' *John Keats: The Complete Poems*, ed. John Barnard, 3rd edn. (Harmondsworth: Penguin, 1988), p. 519.

Portrait of a Scholar

Tight-lipped, the precisian stipples out his thought:
He knows that 'standards' can't be measured by, or 'taught'.
His arrowed admonitions transfix the feeble-hearted,
The strong receive them as a stimulus, imparted
Less from concern to help than from the terror
That prides itself on intolerance of error.
No 'flexible approaches' or 'attitudes' for him;
He keeps his etymologies in trim:
'Radical''s from 'root', *'ramify'* from 'sticks'.
He blanches (white, of course) at metaphors that mix.
And yet, in striving to achieve compression
A cast of lovelessness disfigures his expression.

His accent, purged of local sentiment,
Crisply distinguishes *cóntent* from *contént*.
Unregulated vowel-sounds are his abomination;
He cultivates 'the roll, the rise, the carol, the creation'—[45]
But only so far as the spirit brooks the fetter
Imposed by strict observance of the letter.
The sons of earth command him; he's much cooler
To daughters of Heaven, and beats them with his ruler,[46]
Finding ecstasy only in the daze
Of being knocked senseless by a perfect phrase.

Highly-schooled in common-room politeness,
He trashes ease of mind as ill-bred lightness.
He does not see on brawny backs the dove
Of little unremembered acts of kindness and of love.[47]
Contempt for 'coarseness' has inured him to the graces
That glide and glimmer in the common places.
A slave, not a votary, his skill deserves
A better object than the one it serves:
Fear of failure and a deep suspicion
Of inexplicable departures from tradition.

---

[45] From Gerard Manley Hopkins's poem, 'To R. B.', which begins 'The fine delight that fathers thought'.

[46] 'I am not yet so lost in lexicography, as to forget that words are the daughters of earth, and that things are the sons of heaven.' Dr. Johnson, 'Preface' to his *Dictionary of the English Language* (1755).

[47] '...that best portion of a good man's life, / His little, nameless, unremembered acts / Of kindness and of love.' Wordsworth, 'Lines Composed a Few Miles above 'Tintern Abbey', ll. 34-6.

This phantom lurks in most who toil
To conjure visions from the midnight oil;
Revering force and dignity of language
Too much to stomach rhyming it with *sandwich*.[48]
There's pathos in the zealotry that stops a laugh
When wit essays a moondance in a monograph:
Or mistaking means for ends, principles for rules
Makes of scholarship a ship of fools.
Pathos too, in the quirks of a psychology
That asks admiration for these symptoms of pathology.
A truer wisdom would consent to show
The outlines of the wound in the tension of the bow.[49]

---

[48] Bob Dylan uses this ingeniously imperfect rhyme in his song, 'Sign Language'—given away to Eric Clapton, incidentally: 'You speak to me in sign language / As I'm eating a sandwich / In a small cafe...'

[49] Edmund's Wilson's *The Wound and the Bow* (1941) develops a view, strongly associated with Freud, that creativity arises from the effort to resolve neurotic tension.

Avalanche of Blossom

June: and the slim river suddenly
Full of itself, lolls among the cool
Shades of the elders, nonchalantly spaced
Out along the banks of vivid grass,
Taut with new vitality.

Exams just over and the students have become
What the past three years portended: no
Longer seeds but saplings, root and branch
In lives sown thick with new potential
While the years shine slanting down.

Essays, like the trials they signify,[50]
Are buried in the past for future reference. Loves
And friendships have quickened, sprung
Or sickened as the many souls so beautiful[51]
Make out their own self-image.

And now, still standing here, I watch
Them launching into lives as full of possibility
As the May-trees were,
In Granchester last month
Full of creamy blossom.

---

[50] 'Trials' in the sense of try-outs (*essayer*) and ordeals.
[51] Cp. 'The many men, so beautiful'. 'The Rime of the Ancient Mariner' (1834), l. 236.

The View from Cambridge

Plainly here there are no mountains,
Cwtching up in winter for our warmth;
Or lending memory in spring, my love,
Their shoulders and their slopes to dream upon.

Yet within the level pastures of the sky,
The eye of hope (or is it faith?) can see
Floury fingers of cloud above Fen Ditton[52]
Cracking the sun's soft yolk

Into an old scuffed Pyrex basin
Which became, as I watched you making bakestones,[53] Aunt,
A heart unknowingly full
To breaking with your love.

---

[52] Small village near Cambridge which, in its church tower nestled among trees and secluded by meadows, reminds me of Henllys, east of Risca, whose lovely churchyard was the destination of many Sunday walks.

[53] The local name for what in England (and many parts of Wales) are commonly known as 'Welsh cakes'. (A man selling freshly-made bakestones outdoors in Cardiff told me he thought that anyone using the term 'bakestones' was likely to have learnt it east of the capital). They are traditionally baked on a flat iron slab, which presumably took the place of some earlier 'baking stone'.

To an Absent Therapist

My heart's tired of aching. Christopher Ricks
Has put out a contract on clichés,[54] so instead
My legs tingle. I can hardly sit;
Yet once I stand up, there is nowhere to go.
When I try to write sometimes I feel a twinge
Right in the middle of my groin. Very Freudian?
That's the meet and mindless thing to say.
Pass the *hors d'oeuvres*, super Beaujolais.

Everything bores me. The books in my room
All ask to be read at once, gawping and fluttering
Their pages, like a month-old sparrow.
They can feed them-sodding-selves.
What do they think I am, for God's sake?
A one-man private life-support system?
Aren't they supposed to be supporting *me*?
Precious life-blood of a master-spirit and all that.[55]
Literature's a lousy wet-nurse.

Experience wants me to sip at its cup.
I want one enormous gulp and swallow.
A life's drip-feeding got me where I am
Lying on this page, like a therapist's couch.
Let's get the business over with: food or pain—
Who cares?—so long as it's quick.

There's a fog in my mind. Near the bottom it's so dense
Its feels like a large, flat stone.
Pills dull the ache by deepening the fog
That makes me write these fumbling lines
When I should be springing out flamboyantly
Onto more public stages. My body's amazingly
Stupid—getting ill to tell me I'm screwed up.
I knew that already, o-*kay*?

Let's hope this torment is creative. It could
Save me, if it doesn't kill me first.
And don't worry, I'm not blaming you.
What's the point? Your own secret pain
Has put an electric fence around
The soft part of your sensibility
To keep it safe, like mine.

---

[54] See his excellent essay, 'Clichés'; *The Force of Poetry* (Oxford: Clarendon Press, 1984)

[55] 'A good book is the precious life-blood of a master-spirit, embalmed and treasured up on purpose to a life beyond life' (*Areopagitica*). Milton's dictum was reproduced on the end-papers of many volumes in the original Everyman's Library.

Desert Oak

The sun takes almost an eternity
To leave the endless sky.
All hope, all pleas, all prayers must fade
Like stars, to their own extinction.

Rooted here, from no choice of my own,
First I count the cacti
And then the grains of sand.
But my heart isn't in it.

The sky is so lonely
And the sand goes on for ever.

Only the creaking of my ancient boughs—
As rarely visited by bird or breeze
As by fulfilment of desire—
Reminds me that I am alive

And must watch the sun sink
Beyond my reach
Again and again and again,
Before the earth will take me back,

Resolving me into my elements—
Like a child asleep forever,
Safe in its mother's arms.

Doubling Up

I've got brothers of the flesh and bone
Yet there's another one—
The sibling of a darker self—
Who is my parents' son.

I meet him where desires lock
In silent conflict and caress
The life out of each other's lungs
Through years of gentle stress.

He knows me for an ally; knows
I'll never cast him out:
His face distinct from mine no more
Than echo is from shout

I touch my arm, but I can't feel
The texture of my skin
Except where numbness lends a hand
To let sensation in.

I search the mirror's surface, try
To see my image neutrally
But looking at, and with, my eye
Disguises 'it' in 'me'.

This brother of my other self
Is strong, but less resilient
Than what he labours to oppress
Yet keeps alive in torment.

He made a mantle for me, bade
Me wear it, most persuasively;
But slowly as it seared my flesh
I felt it wasn't me:

Felt that the life I lived belonged
To him and wronged my spirit;
That endless striving for his goal
Had brought me nowhere near it.

Distinct, but far too insecure
For triumph, in these acts of time
I glimpse the outlines of the play
That will supplant the pantomime.

I dare not let my self presume
It knows itself too well to know
Which firstlings of a truer life
Retain the sap to grow.

Only the impulse quickening
My pen in watches of the night
Affords me shy assurances
The poem will come right.

Daybreak

Head in his hands like a crystal ball;
Eyes fast-curtained and the night drawn in;
Chilled with uncertainty, a mist of tears
Dissolves its pattern on the pavement of his heart.

High above it all the stars revolve the question
In the womby blackness of the lost Welsh night;
They shine with yearning for illumination,
But cleave to habits that perplex the light.

The morning is so usual, the bathroom feels
Properly indifferent to diurnal pain:
The mirror reflects no particular despair:
He writes the poem while he cleans his teeth.

Sulk

Dispiriting to see these dates beside
Poems I read ten years ago:
Troubled then, still troubled now.
Few palpable gains and the pencil marks are fading.

I plan books I refuse to write.
I proclaim my impotence from the stanza-tops,
Inviting someone—parent, doctor, colleague—
To help with my re-birth, or attend the next miscarriage.

I shoot up on self-sabotage. If I fail,
They'll see the harm they've done me. However,
God doesn't oblige, but labours at his desk
Of dreams, hoping to quicken me into imitation.

I must bestir myself. This prosy poem
Isn't work exactly, though being pedestrian
Might be a first step towards free-wheeling through the planets;
Might still convert my cribbed and moth-balled psyche,

Metal-jacketed through years of thwarted vengefulness
Into a chrysalis; might just relax
The habit of despair around some muse's throat, and
Blessing me with impulse, let me sing myself free.

Modern Prayer

Strike lightning through my brain.
Cleave my defences apart.
Let me be born again.
Galvanize my heart.[56]

Yet... gather me up in peace
Cosset my soul in sweet balms,
Lap me and love me and hold me
Safe in your mothering arms.

The mid-points along the scale
From fury to tenderness
Are muffled and skewed in my throat
I register them less

Than extremes of emotion—fear
And longing and loss and despair—
Which run through my dreams like a fever,
And leave on my outlook a scar.

Minds play the devil with hope:
Their very imperfections
Ensure that attempts at self-cure
Propagate new infections.

Time goes maundering on
And suffering seems here to stay.
I yearn for something like grace
As I lie on your couch to pray.

---

[56] See Donne's famous sonnet, 'Batter my heart, three-personed God...'

Secularism

Lachrimae antiquae novae:[57]
These inward tears have been shed before
But never as now has their salt seeped
Into wounds less apt to heal and sore.

Back from Christmas shopping,
There's a piece to write (we need more cash);
How else supply our vacancies
Except with quasi-spiritual stash?

Alone after the argument,
Which ran like an oily river through
Each innocent field of conversation,
I compose myself and renew

Acquaintance with Dowland's lute,
Which pleased my young man's woe,[58]
And quaff the fall of cadences
That taste of where they used to flow.

It was talking about the local streets
That did the damage: how those boot-scrapers
Were needed for the mud that clung
To lives far needier than ours.

But only perhaps in some things.
Spoilt with choice we can't shun or cure,
We collect consumer durables
In a world where they, no more than we, endure.

---

[57] 'Old tears renewed'. Title of a song by John Dowland (1562-1626).
[58] Cp. 'My mirth it much displeased, but pleased my woe'. *Measure for Measure*, 4:1:13

Fireworks

'Pretty! Pretty! Look! Isn't is pretty?'
The question and elation are unreal.
Standing on a bridge, this Cambridge mother
In Aquascutum and co-ordinated scarf
Isn't so much expressing joy as schooling
Her upheld daughter in the protocols of praise.
She whooshes with desire to make her little girl
Not good, necessarily, but nice: the sort
Who'll take a pleasure in home cooking (*chez lui*),
Selecting her ingredients, and her guests, with care.

Touched off, my prejudices smoulder, launch and writhe.
Years of wilful temperance reel back before
A coruscating hydra of assumptions. I suspect
This woman's house is honorifically unkempt;
She votes Lib. Dem.; knows the value of
An Oxbridge education; no doubt can ride
Any intelligent hobbyhorse, though she rears
Up when the going gets—well, you know, *unpleasant*.
She'd be glowingly adept at demure dissimulation
Should a less advantaged person make the gaffe
Of being too nakedly, vulgarly intent
Upon a game of darts or skittles; yet,
Having an educated sensibility, she'd avow,
Aver, perhaps asseverate, indeed,
The intellectual virtue of 'openness'.

Thank God there's a province
Far from whatever my meanness means
Where the sky is hung with axioms which
Derive their universal status
From better predilections than my own.
It's need that burnishes the platitudes
Of bourgeois secular humanism till
They throb like stars in the one enlightened
Corner of our sublunary world.
What price the aspect of eternity when
We enjoy the auspices of self-esteem?

The liberal consensus is a fountain of good sense
If it isn't a Roman candle of complacencies
Or an unexploded mortar of origin obscure
Looking for a psyche to go off in.

I sympathise enough with her to know
Smugness like rage is a symptom of despair.
She'd choose to pay, with Larkin, for first class
So as to keep from yobs beyond redemption.
She stops her nose because she cannot stop
The miasma rising from morality's corpse,
The rattle rising in a culture's shallow throat.

And yet more deeply still I sympathise
With Mrs C.'s young daughter. Twenty years
From now I see her stand here on the bridge
That links vulgarity and gentility,[59]
Unable to speak to some sixty-year-old fellow-
Watcher of the fireworks. Ill-read in the eloquence
Of social gesture, her face not knowing how to form
A candid smile, she mutters murderously to herself,
In pronunciation helplessly received,
'Pretty! Pretty! Pull the damn things down!'—
In a flash her whole sensibility implodes
In pyrotechnic imitation of
The anger she is dumb with.

                    That night she 'phones her mother. 'Oh,
The fireworks? Yes, Mum, Jessica and I
Thought them pretty (didn't we?), very, very pretty.'

[59] The railway bridge in question is on Mill Road in Cambridge. It marks a division, in estate
agents' terms, between the better and the worse side of the tracks (Petersfield and Romsey).

Lesson

So little remains
Beyond the shrinking absurdity
Of her surname: Wrintmore, Miss of course—
Her forename locketed in secrecy
Deeper than a bedroom sigh. Far off
She taught ageless children
In a Risca school, which (like herself)
No longer stands. Her hair
Curled tight and grey around a face
Whose premature rubescence some
Cheap powder from a trip
To Newport had subdued;
Her dresses always
Spotless, always
To our indifferent eyes undiffering,
Sported their faded floral prints
Like a meadow making the best of itself
Although no lovers slept there.

I don't remember
A single word she said. Her lips
Move soundlessly above the decades.
Yet one afternoon she gave
A reprimand which ripens to
An intuition.

It was sultry, maybe summer,
And the light slunk dull
Across our heavy-lidded
Desks. She'd set us
Silent reading (then a special sort,
With something of the atmosphere of chapel) and,
Because I couldn't brook it long, she told me
To tell a visiting teacher what I'd read.
Something about a collie, it was.
Probably I limbered up cautiously, one eye
Wary of a clip, but soon
I loped into a cocky frisk
And romped, explaining, home.

I never knew
Whether I'd distinguished or disgraced myself;
And only now, a lifetime later, understand
What Miss Wrintmore was teaching me:
The taste of lonely afternoons,
Oppressed by childhoods full of promises
(In her case broken or forgotten),
When she'd gazed
Across a tousled, sunlit field
And seen flushed lovers saunter and felt
Between the heavy beatings of her heart a swell
Of something that compounded
Memory and desire,
And loss beyond appeasement
Which poems far away
In London wouldn't entertain.

It has taken time
To write a hundred lines across my own desires,
Meeting themselves scuffed and
Tearful coming back,
For me to understand the lesson which
She spent her life learning
How to teach.

Elder Wine

I love the elder: how it *is* a tree
And yet for love of rural harmony
Consents to be a bush. When young,
It hardly holds together: branches sprung
In surly nonchalance aside, as though
The need for solidarity took time to grow.
Its flowers aren't ashamed of seeming crude:
Cow-parsley with a bit of attitude,
But no pretence of purity: they dream
Of nothing whiter than their froth of cream
Tinged with greenness, lest they drift apart
From origins they'd rather keep to heart.

Their perfume is a dank enchantment, some
Recoil from its suggestion of a plant that's come
To deep fruition in the sun's embraces
Thickening the air with musky traces.
This Arabella of the shade, in June
Expends her spirit in a noontide swoon,
And lets her flowers be ravaged in a waste
Of winds which reel and stagger from the taste
Of so much rank vitality. Her hair
Love-tousled now, casts upon the air
Its shattered creamy coronets, until
She falls asleep and autumn has its will.

It is, of course, like everything a symbol:
Of loves which living makes us leave behind
Or carry lightly in solution, like the wine
We dreamt each year of squeezing from the fronds
Of elder in the yard where my first bonds
Were tied and loosed: more perfect wine
Than ever burst upon a palate fine
Or crude (as ours were, doubtless); yet
Wine so perfect I will not forget
Its ideal savour. It ferments in me
A longing for perfections I will never see.

The elder, rooted in a soil that's cursed
To disappoint, sets me athirst
For joys as heavenly as earthy: blisses
We taste obscurely in a lover's kisses.[60]

---

[60] This rhyme and indeed the form and feel of the whole poem were suggested by Keats's *Endymion* ('Those lips, O slippery blisses'—Book 2, line 760). The phrase 'palate fine' is from 'Ode to Melancholy', where the image of somebody bursting 'Joy's grape against his palate fine' implies that melancholy and joy are part of each other.

Love Children

Suddenly she re-assumes the child:
Her face is overcome with playgrounds where
Hostilities, like bits of toys and love
Misprised, were scorchingly exchanged;

Her eyes give into her mother's house,
(Best friends departed) while she stands forlorn
Among discarded fairy-cakes, and feels
The stream of disappointment swell.

It bursts the banks of her composure.
Pangs from underneath the mattresses
Of memories laid down years ago
Disturb her anguish in its sleep:

Her father in a sports car, driving off
Into oblivion, his raffishness
Inscribed in movements that still turn her head,
His accents in the voices that entrance her heart;

Her lover on a morning unexceptional
In everything except it was his last,
Saying 'See you later' as he closed the door
That led, unknowing, to abandonment

And me, distraught among the suds
Of agonies I have washed too clean,
Struggling to fashion an embrace
Our childhoods might make love in.

Time's Coat

For Judy

It might have been in Camden Town
Some winter night, snow lazing down,
Lights in the trees, love in our eyes,
Time on our side, though we know that it flies.

That mike-stand you gave me, to sing out my song—
I lean on it still and hope it lasts long.
That bracelet of silver and amethyst
Unchanging, encircles your delicate wrist.

The old roads of London wind up the hill.
We stroll through the crowds and feel we stand still.
The lads are out drinking, there's fights in the yard:
It's years that'll teach them the meaning of 'hard'.

I tighten my grip, feel the bones of your hand,
I know that we slip, as we're trying to stand.
Times like this I need your kiss...
Holding my fear in the form that I'd miss.

The dance and step of your feminine graces...
Time will make Halloween masks of our faces.
We need a word, call it a soul,
For whatever it is burns to last, like coal.

Music swirls between the girls and guys in Camden Town.
Christmas drifts through subtle shifts of memory lazily down.
Time's like a coat, it's warm, but it's wearing:
We'll take it off, love, when we've learnt to be daring.

Catching Gold

The spent rudd rolled
His golden slab
Of flank palm-flat
Towards the sun.

The silver sheet
Of surface shimmered
Like a breaking dream
Above his punch-drunk eye.

Played out, his lolling loveliness
Of movement yielding
To a leaden slump,
From side to weary side,

He let me pluck—
As I hove him into
The neon white
Of my dry, prose world—

Just a shard, just a shiver,
Just the glimmer of a gift
From the heart
Of his fishy mystery.

Talents [61]

Two coins I buried in the ground,
Then watered it with tears
To find if twenty watchful years
Would prove the banking sound.

Meanwhile the warlocks of the wood
Plotted to steal my heart away;
Machen and Twmbarlwm lay
Hourly siege upon my blood. [62]

The waters of the Deeps [63] sank through
The ancient strata of my brain;
The trees along the bank through pain
Of loss took root in me and grew.

The settee where my Uncle chose
To take 'fiesta' (meaning nap),
Ached to have him in its lap
Once he slept where the bluebell blows.

The chair beside it where my Aunt
In grief and laughter rocked herself
While the clock on the mantle-shelf
Ticked on, would comfort her, but can't.

I gaze into the gas fire, hear
The axe split stick, the bulbous hammer
Clunk apart the coal. The grammar
Of experience is untransformed each year.

The television screen is bare:
Its pupil has engulfed its eye;
Yet stars above the Risca sky
Remain in focus everywhere.

I reach into my head, remove
A few small coins from the teeming earth.
I try to weigh what they are worth
By telling what they prove.

---

[61] See the Biblical story of the talents in *Matthew*, 25:14-29. The word originally denoted a coin, which, through the parable, was understood as something you were given but needed to invest shrewdly so as to maximise its value. The modern sense of the term 'talent' is thus an ability that's latent until you are able to develop it.

[62] Both these mountains, and their names, were prominent in my childhood and remain so in my imagination.

[63] A section of the Monmouthshire canal above Risca, where as a boy I spent hundreds of hours fishing.

Turning Verse

Somewhere back beyond the pale
That hems the lighted, broken ground
Of consciousness, a shovel sinks
Into the leafmould of the mind.

It scoops a molten hundredweight
Of meanings on its polished blade:
A rich molass of vocables,
Compressed through years of dream and wake.

A voice takes hold of the shovel's haft
And lugs its trove into the sun;
Then lets it slither on the ground
To spell a syntax if it can.

Acknowledgements

Since this collection is so largely an expression of love and gratitude towards particular people, naming them all here might be superfluous. My mother, Wendy Logan, isn't directly named in any of these poems, but without her belief in the value of education it's possible that none of them would have been written. The vitality which I've always sought in my creative work and personal life was a very highly developed trait in her and in the culture we both come from. For that and very much else, she has all my love and gratitude. My father was a singer, giving me faith in the value of song. I am indebted to him beyond words.

There have been many who, in their different ways, have encouraged me as a poet. Among these I would like to thank in particular Roger Farrington, poet and magistrate, who taught me at The Working Men's College and has been a close friend ever since; Geoff Pawling, poet and painter, my best boss, who was uniquely gifted in the appreciation of the gifts of others; Brendan Kennelly, poet, for telling me, early on, that he thought 'Time's Coat' a genuine poem; Seamus Heaney, for assuring me that the story in these poems was worth telling; Jan Morris, for showing that the mountain may occasionally bow to the molehill and sending me a fan letter; Julie Morrison, for hoping so ardently that *Heartlands* would be published and seeing its relation to my albums; Steve Cannon, for designing the Moondragon logo; Sharon and Steve Mather, Dave Pescod and Kate Rhodes, for helping me believe my poems might have value; Stephen Gill, for reading some of my earliest poems and taking them seriously; Christopher Ricks, for writing about some even earlier ones and finding a way to be critical that was still encouraging; Steve Fleetwood for pinning a poem of mine on his study wall; Wynn Thomas, for helping me to get my first poems published and for educating me, as he does still, in the complexities of Welsh identity; Meic Stephens for showing me that Welsh writing in English was a vast and beautiful wilderness; Iwan Bala, painter, for bothering to praise my poems after a reading at Gregynog; Pamela Petro, writer, for valuing both my prose about hiraeth and the poems that express it; my sister Sarah and brother-in-law Mike Logan, for their loving support of my work in poetry and music; Patrick Jones, poet and playwright, for giving me a warm sense of solidarity in our shared creative purposes; Peter Lomas, psychotherapist, for responding to my poems as though they were worth all the nurturing he gave them. Poets are known for writing poems. But poetry is a making, a bringing to life of something good that didn't exist before. All these people, in words or otherwise, are poets.

I am grateful to Nick and John Garrad and Kathryn Preston, for collaborating with me so generously in the physical design and production of the book; to Michèle Smith for her work in promoting it and to Julianne Ingles for introducing me to Michèle.

Several of the poems in *Heartlands* have appeared in *The Swansea Review* and in *Planet: The Welsh Internationalist*. I am grateful for permission to reprint.

And finally I thank my wife Judy Logan, painter and muse. I wrote the earliest poem in this collection sitting opposite her in Bewley's cafe, Dublin. She has from the first put the heart into all my poems and songs and then has helped it sing.